QUICK
&EASY massage

DUNCAN BAIRD PUBLISHERS

LONDON

QUICK & EASY massage

Beata Aleksandrowicz

5-minute massages for

anyone
anytime
anywhere

QUICK & EASY massage

Beata Aleksandrowicz

Distributed in the USA and Canada by
Sterling Publishing Co., Inc.
387 Park Avenue South, New York, NY 10016-8810

This edition first published in the UK in 2008 and in the USA in 2009 by
Duncan Baird Publishers Ltd
Sixth Floor, Castle House, 75–76 Wells Street, London W1T 3QH

Managing Editor: Grace Cheetham
Editor: Judith More
Managing Designer: Manisha Patel
Designer: Jantje Doughty
Commissioned photography: Jules Selmes

Library of Congress Cataloging-in-Publication Data

Aleksandrowicz, Beata.
   Quick & easy massage : 5-minute massage for anyone anytime anywhere / Beata
Aleksandrowicz.
      p. cm.
   Includes index.
   ISBN 978-1-84483-839-4
   1. Massage. I. Title. II. Title: Quick and easy massage.
   RA780.5.A44 2008
   615.8'22--dc22

                                        2009000862

ISBN: 978-1-84483-839-4
10 9 8 7 6 5 4 3 2 1

Typeset in Gill Sans, Nofret and Helvetica Neue
Color reproduction by Scanhouse, Malaysia
Printed in China by Imago

For information about custom editions, special sales, premium and corporate
purchases, please contact Sterling Special Sales Department at 800-805-5489
or specialsales@sterlingpub.com.

To my Mum and my Dad
– who loved me as much
as they could

contents

6   introduction

anytime

22   morning wake-up
24   shower time
26   lunchtime lift
28   evening de-stress
30   lazy weekend
32   take a moment
34   before a meeting
36   at a conference

anywhere

40   in your bedroom
42   in your bathroom
44   on your sofa
46   at the park
48   at the beach
50   at your desk
52   in a hotel room
54   on a plane

stress busters

58   scalp lifter
60   lower back reliever
62   body relaxer
64   eye calmer
66   jaw reliever
68   foot de-stresser
70   neck balancer

mood enhancers

74   chest booster
76   foot reviver
78   face lifter
80   abdominal soother
82   head booster
84   neck warmer
86   sinus clearer

energy boosters

90   shoulder stretcher
92   face booster
94   neck reviver
96   thigh booster
98   ear reviver
100   back releaser
102   body energizer

practising together

106   getting connected
108   letting go
110   back relaxer
112   working together
114   sleep enhancer
116   touching hands
118   caring for feet
120   balancing touch
122   tension reliever

124   everyday sequences

126   index/acknowledgments

introduction

This is a book for everybody — whatever your age, you will enjoy the proven healing benefits of all the massage sequences included and find the step-by-step approach easy to follow. All the techniques I share with you in this book are simple, yet these short rituals can make a big difference to your life, because they give you tools to reach out to others. Through touch, we communicate.

the healing touch

It was such a joy for me to work on this project because I strongly believe in the importance of massage in daily life — massage is so much more than just a once-a-year pampering treatment in a spa. Touch, the mother of all senses, can not only heal the aches and pains in our bodies caused by physical activities or stress, but also nourish our souls when we feel lonely, anxious, depressed or hurt.

In my everyday work, I experience the instant, often significant and wide-ranging effects, of massage. Based on the feedback from my clients, I know that massage doesn't just alleviate physical pain. After receiving a massage, my clients also feel more relaxed, positive, respected, appreciated and uplifted.

The physiological benefits of massage are well-known: muscles are toned and firmer, posture improves, the nervous system is more

6

balanced, the respiratory system is strengthened, the hormonal system is rebalanced, blood circulation is increased, and the skin is smoother and firmer. Massage encourages the lymph flow, which carries all waste products from the body so we can function more healthily, our immune system is strengthened, and our energy level lifts.

In my practice, I don't associate massage with pampering and all the luxury paraphernalia that it has been linked to in recent times. From its earliest inception, massage was intended as a healing art. Children in pain understand this instinctively: they come to their parents to soothe their hurt and we give them a little rub and a good word to make them feel better. Last century, nurses massaged soldiers to ease the wounds of war. And today, seriously ill patients, including AIDS and cancer sufferers, benefit from massage. Massage treatment reduces anxiety by helping to slow down the heart rate and relieve stress. It also reduces pain by releasing the well-being hormone, seratonin, and providing emotional comfort.

Touch is also a very powerful communication tool. I experienced this during a visit to the bushmen of the Kalahari Desert, in Namibia. I was among people who didn't speak my language, whose lives were completely different to mine, and yet we were able to create deep, profound contact through touch.

7

On the massage courses I run, I often tell participants that if they have an emotional moment when they don't know what to say, they should use touch instead. For example, just a light touch on the arm or hand will bring much-needed comfort and a feeling of support to a bereaved person, when words may not flow easily.

who benefits from massage?

This book takes you through different situations in everyday life where you can use massage – either on yourself, or to help a partner, child, parent or friend – to relieve physical and emotional tension.

The educational aspect of the book is very important to me as I believe that massage can be taught to everybody, and more importantly can be used in every moment of our hectic lives. As recent research studies show, general stress levels are rising, making a healing touch a daily necessity.

In the baby massage course I run, I have observed how crying babies respond positively to touch, and calm down. Recent studies have shown that babies develop faster, and that their mothers develop better communication with them, if they are massaged regularly.

For seniors, too, I believe that touch is crucial as they can feel rejected, or embarrassed by their age and the changes that have

8

taken place in their bodies. I am convinced that if you can give your grandmother or grandfather, or your mother or father, a soothing neck or a hand massage, it can make a world of difference in their life.

With teenagers, who generally avoid any sort of communication, massage can be a way for another member of the family to listen to their emotions, and soothe their pains.

And for couples, a simple foot or hand massage at bedtime is a caring gesture that builds trust and understanding. It is a wonderful non-verbal expression of their bond, and will reassure both partners that they are important to each other.

I want this book to help you to believe in yourself, and in your abilities to massage. In its pages I set out to show you that you don't have to be vulnerable when confrontating physical or emotional pain, and to teach you how you can help yourself and others using this time-honoured, natural self-healing method.

I also would like to encourage you to share your touch with others. To help you to achieve this I have created a final chapter that includes "each-other" massage techniques. If you follow the instructions in this chapter, and you trust in yourself, you can master these techniques and share them with others. Massage is such a great way to communicate with those you share your life with.

10

The techniques in chapter 6 can be shared between husband and wife, children and parents, or friends. They give you a chance to communicate through touch, and teach you helpful massage sequences you can use to express caring feelings to all those who are close to you. You should always try to give your massage partner the best massage you can, and never refuse to give one – for tomorrow it might be you who will be asking for a much-needed healing touch.

Be aware that massage is a giving and receiving process, and from my experience there is an equal distribution of energy between the giver and the receiver. Therefore, you should always try to exchange massages equally. That said, however, it is a good habit to agree that the person who is more tense or tired should receive their massage first. The reason for this lies in the fact that we transmit all our emotions and thoughts with our touch, therefore it is important that your mind is relaxed, and is filled with positive thoughts and emotions, while you are offering massage to somebody. else

Massage is of great benefit to most people. However, there are some cases where it is not appropriate. For a list of the basic contra-indications you must take into account before you start any massage, see the list on pages 13–14. If in doubt, I would recommend that you ask your general practitioner if massage is suitable for you.

11

contra-indications

If you fall into one of these categories you should avoid massage:

• You have a high temperature. Massage stimulates the body's metabolism, and can cause the temperature to rise even higher. You can still use touch of course! We all know the blissful sensation of somebody's cold hand on our forehead when we are sick.

• It is less than an hour since you ate a large meal. Don't use massage techniques on a full stomach, to prevent pressure on inner organs.

• You have had a recent injury or an accident that caused open wounds, bruising, or fractures. In such cases, you should always take professional advice before embarking on a massage.

• You have a serious lower back problem, persistent back or neck pain, or any other significant body restriction. If this is the case, you should go to an osteopath to check out the cause of the problem and discuss massage options with him or her.

• You are pregnant. If you are pregnant, you should massage your lower back and abdomen very gently during the first three months. You must also take professional advice regarding the oils you use, as some essential oils are unsuitable for pregnant women.

• If you have varicose veins, avoid any direct pressure on affected veins, and keep any pressure very light around such an area.

a time and a place

You may wonder how it's possible to find time for even a simple, short massage. We all need more time, and most of us think that our day is too short. We often postpone time for ourselves –"me-time" – to the following day. To solve this problem, I have based the massage treatments in this book around natural breaks that you can find in your everyday activities. Your quick-and-easy massage session won't interfere with your day in any way, but rather give you strength, and enable you to enjoy your free time in a more relaxed manner.

I've suggested ideas for using massage techniques in almost every circumstance: during a long flight, in the shower, at your desk, or resting on the beach. You will also find techniques that will help you to release stress or add energy to your life, or help you to enhance your mood. You can use this book anytime and anywhere: at home, in the office, at the hospital. My aim is to prove that you can use massage in everyday life. You don't need any special preparation, and you don't have to be a qualified massage therapist to soothe neck pain, or to comfort your loved one. On the other hand, it is important to say that the book is not a replacement for professional massage.

My wish is also to show you that you don't have to feel powerless when confronting pain – your own or another's. You can help your

14

body and your mind in the most ancient and natural way. If you don't know what to say, or do, then just touch.

golden rules

There are some key rules to follow if you want to get the maximum benefit from this book. Please read these carefully before you begin.

- **Breathing well.** You should regard breathing as an internal massage of all your organs. When you take an in-breath, your lungs expand, pushing on the diaphragm, which causes a cascade effect on all the organs below, including your stomach, liver, and kidneys. This happens because they are all attached to each other through the connective tissue, therefore whatever movement takes place in one organ, the others are affected. Breathing fills your lungs with oxygen, which is then transferred to your blood cells, and these carry the oxygen around your body. Very often, feelings of fatigue, headaches, impaired vision, and poor motor coordination are caused by incorrect breathing.

- **Staying silent.** It is important that you don't talk during massage. That way, you can switch off your mind, as a kind of mental break, refreshing your whole system. Some of the techniques in this book can be carried out at home, where it is obviously easier to follow the rule of silence. If you are in a public place, you'll need to be

15

more disciplined in order to switch off and tune in with yourself. Use deep, regular breathing as your guide. Concentrate purely on your breathing for two or three minutes before you start self-massage, to help you to switch off your mind.

- **Getting the pressure right.** If you listen to your body carefully, it will tell you if the pressure is wrong. Pain usually signifies that you are using pressure that is too strong or too fast. Lighten up immediately, and slow the movement down. Apply pressure gradually, rather than pushing suddenly. In all techniques that require static pressure, trust your intuition to locate the sore spots. With practice, you will become more and more aware of the tension that is always present in a sore spot as a result of the build-up of waste products (mostly toxins that haven't been removed by the circulation). Avoid direct pressure on the bones, especially when you are working along the spine. Always concentrate pressure on the muscles.

- **Finding the right rhythm and speed.** Practice making slow movements. Imagine that you are walking through a city that you have never seen before. If you run, you can't experience anything fully. You need time and awareness to assimilate as much as possible from an unknown place. The same is true of the human body. Discover it slowly and carefully through the process of touch. The more

16

you are present, the more natural the slow speed of massage will become. Keep a steady rhythm as you work, and make at least as many repetitions as I have suggested in the book. By making these rhythmical, repetitive movements you are helping your nervous system to relax and restore the natural balance of your body.

how to use this book

You can start to try massage from any page: the book is structured in such a way that it is easy for you to use every day. I have made sure that all the techniques featured are simple enough for beginners. All you need is your desire to connect with yourself, or with the other person you will be massaging. Always begin by breathing deeply several times, with closed eyes, to relax both body and mind.

I believe that this book will become your trusty companion, not only as a source of remedies for aches and pains, but also because it can make every moment in your life a bit more meaningful through the transforming power of touch. I hope that by using this book you will become as passionate about massage as I am, and that this book will bring joy into your life – the joy of giving and receiving touch.

19

anytime

You can put massage techniques to work at any convenient moment

to release tension and make you feel better. In the morning, massage is

a great preparation for the challenges of the day, while in the evening

there is no better way to relax both body and mind.

1 Sit on the side of the bed, with your feet touching the floor. Relax your arms and make sure that you have a good connection between your feet and the surface underneath. Place your hands on your lap and close your eyes. Take a deep, slow breath. Gently, without any force, breathe out. Repeat three times.

2 (*right*) Put your right hand on your scalp, while the left one rests on your lap. Comb your fingers through the roots of your hair, close to the forehead, and close your fist. Grasp as much hair as you can, take a deep breath and, while breathing out, pull gently on the hair. Keep your fist very close to your scalp. Release.

3 While taking another in-breath, reposition your right hand toward the back of your scalp, grasp as much hair as you can, and pull gently with the out-breath. Continue pulling and releasing hair over the whole right side of your scalp. Pull firmly and rhythmically, so you can feel your scalp move. Use your left hand to work on the left side of your scalp.

4 Place the fingers of both hands on your head and tap gently all over the scalp, breathing regularly. Imagine that heavy rain drops are falling on your head. Increase the speed of the tapping motion until you feel a pleasant warmth spreading all over your scalp. If you prefer, you can use relaxed fists, tapping gently, as an alternative to your fingers.

22

morning wake-up
invigorating

awaken physically and mentally when
you haven't had enough sleep

shower time
connecting
an ideal time to give yourself a very effective massage

1 Make sure that the water is hot enough to make you feel warm. Before you apply soap, stand quietly under the shower and feel the water pouring over your body, massaging it gently. Close your eyes, breathe deeply, and enjoy this very relaxing and soothing sensation.

2 Apply soap over your arms, shoulders, chest and neck, working up a lather. Make both your hands into loose fists, and start to roll your knuckles over your chest. The soap will encourage your fingers to slide without any resistance. Take care to avoid your collarbone, and work just on the chest area below it.

3 Place your right hand on your left arm at the elbow and make invigorating circles, sliding your hand up your arm. When you reach the shoulder, slide back down your arm to the elbow in one movement. Repeat three times, then make five energetic circles on your left shoulder. Change hands, then massage the opposite arm and shoulder in the same way.

4 (*opposite*) Make loose fists with both hands, and place them on the base of your neck. Roll your knuckles along the base of your neck, then up both sides to the base of your scalp. Come back to your starting point, knuckling the back of your neck from the base of the scalp down to the shoulders. Repeat three times. Finish the shower with lukewarm water.

25

1 Sit comfortably, with your feet touching the floor, and close your eyes. If you prefer to stand, relax your shoulders and don't lock your knees. Breathe deeply and regularly, concentrating on your breathing, to energize your body, and also give your mind a quick rest.

2 (*right*) Very slowly, lift your shoulders as high as you can, keeping your arms straight and loose. Do this gradually, with your in-breath. Any resistance in your shoulders will decrease with more repetitions. Don't force the movement, and lift only as high as is comfortable for you.

3 Hold your shoulders as high as possible for two slow in-breaths. With an out-breath, very slowly slide them down as low as you can, trying not to push, but rather releasing the muscles. Repeat three times. Each time, more space will open up between your shoulders and neck.

4 Place your right hand on your left shoulder socket, take an in-breath, and, while breathing out. rotate your hand inward over the socket, using fast, rhythmical movements. Breathe in again, then, while breathing out, make five outward rotations over the socket.

Change hands, and repeat this fast, rhythmical circling with your left hand over your right shoulder. Open your eyes, and breathe deeply.

lunchtime lift
energizing
restore your energy in the middle of the day

evening de-stress soothing

a great way to finish the day and improve your sleeping pattern

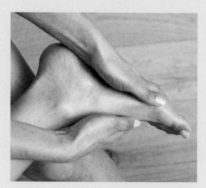 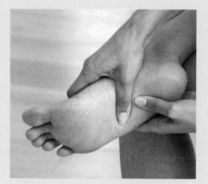

1 You can either sit on a chair or on the edge of the bed. Relax and rest your right foot on your left knee. Slowly and gently, apply cream to the top and sole of your foot. Sandwich your foot between your hands, and make circles with both hands all over the foot, starting from your toes and sliding toward your ankle.

2 Place both thumbs on the top of the sole, with fingers supporting the top of your foot. Press both thumbs into the sole and make three outward, deep, slow circles. Lift and move your thumbs to another point on your sole, press again, and make another three outward circles. Work all over sole and heel, taking care to breathe regularly.

ANYTIME

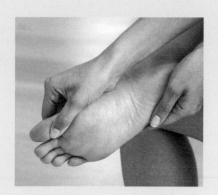

3 Cup your heel in the palm of your left hand for support. Press your right thumb into your big toe. Make five slow circles in both directions, working on the whole surface of your big toe. Move to each of your other toes in turn and repeat the circles.

4 Now supporting your foot with your right hand, press your left thumb into the middle, top point of the sole. Slide down along this middle line to the edge of your heel, using your left thumb. Hold your foot between both hands, breathing deeply three times. Finally, repeat the massage sequence in steps 1–4 on your left foot.

29

lazy weekend
pampering

relax your hands and leave them looking firm and fresh

1 Sit comfortably on the sofa, supporting your back with a pillow and keeping your legs straight, knees supported. Apply hand cream to the back and fingers of your right hand, using slow movements and covering the hand to the wrist. Stroke from fingers to wrist several times, then apply cream to your right palm.

2 (*opposite*) Rest your right hand on the fingers of your left hand, palm up. Using the thumb of your left hand, slide along the tendons, from the knuckle of your little finger toward the wrist. Repeat between every finger, working each time from the knuckle toward the wrist.

3 Squeeze the base of the little finger of your right hand between the thumb and index fingers of your left hand, and make circles around the finger, working up to the fingernail. Repeat on each finger three times, breathing slowly and keeping your shoulders relaxed.

4 Massage the palm of your right hand with the thumb of your left hand, using the fingers of the left hand as support. Make small circles with your thumb all over the palm. You should feel the tension releasing. Finish by holding both hands together and breathing deeply three times. Repeat steps 1–4 once more, this time on your other hand.

31

take a moment focusing

release tension, to leave you alert and refreshed

1 Standing in front of a mirror will help you to control the position of every movement. Start by taking three deep breaths. Stroke one hand after another up your forehead, into the hairline, five times. Relax your hands and make sure that the movement is slow, but rhythmical. Take care that you don't apply too much pressure.

2 Place the fingers of both hands over your forehead. Press slowly into the skin, using the finger pads, and make five outward, slow, regular circles. Try not to just stretch the skin – think about creating slow movements of the tissue underneath. Make sure that you cover the whole forehead, including the hairline and above the eyebrows.

3 Hold both your hands across your forehead and press in with the index and middle fingers. Make a "zig-zag" stroke, moving both hands toward each other. Start slowly, then gradually increase the speed, before slowing down again. Work all over the forehead for 30 seconds.

4 Place the ring and middle finger of your right hand on the bridge of your nose, between your eyebrows, and take an in-breath. Rest your left hand in your lap. Make light circles in a spiral movement, sliding along the middle line of the forehead from the base of the nose up to the hairline. Breathe deeply, keeping your shoulders relaxed.

33

before a meeting
balancing

energize and give yourself a sense of harmony

1 Place one hand on top of each shoulder, with palms facing down. Firmly embrace the muscles that lie on top of the shoulder and connect to the neck. Breathing out slowly, squeeze and lift your shoulders in your hands, and hold. On the next out-breath, release your grip slowly. Repeat three times, lifting and holding each time.

2 Form fists and place them on the top of each shoulder. On the out-breath, tap vigorously and rhythmically along the muscular part of your shoulders. Make sure that your hands don't slide onto the bone, which might be painful. Breathe regularly, and continue tapping for 15 seconds.

3 Gently place one hand on each shoulder, with your palms facing down. Close your eyes, and feel a comforting warmth emanating from your shoulders. Imagine "sending" your breath toward your shoulders.

4 Place one hand on either side of your head. On the out-breath, press gently into the scalp and hold. Breathe in. With another out-breath, release the pressure, feeling the warmth of your hands on your scalp. Repeat three times. Open your eyes.

35

1 Make sure that you are sitting straight, legs uncrossed and feet connecting with the floor. Take off your shoes if possible. Relax your shoulders and bend your neck slightly forward to reduce any tension in it. You need to be aware that if you bend your neck too much you will cause additional resistance, instead of helping your muscles to relax.

2 (*right*) Place your right hand on your left shoulder. Breathe deeply, feeling the hand's warmth spreading over the shoulder. Press your index and middle fingers into the muscle without changing position, and, with an out-breath, make as many slow, deep circles as you wish. If the spot is sore, press into the muscle and just hold for several breaths.

3 Work along the shoulder, selecting the most tender spots and massaging them using either circular or static pressure. Start with slow, deep circles, then increase the speed. With your left hand, work on the other shoulder, repeating steps 1–3.

4 Place both hands on your lap, bring your head back upright, and rotate your shoulders five times backward and five times forward, keeping your neck relaxed. Make sure that you don't bend your elbows or use your lower arms; you should feel the movement starting from the shoulder. Breathe deeply three times.

at a **conference**
refreshing
maintain your mind and body energy during demanding events

anywhere

You don't have to go to a spa to experience the benefits of massage.

You can apply simple techniques wherever you are, to help you relax,

to boost your energy, or to ease tension or minor pains.

in your bedroom
de-stressing

relax your lower back and relieve stress-related pain

1 Lie on your right side. Keeping your bottom leg straight, bend your upper leg and fold it over the bottom leg, so that the top ankle rests over the bottom knee. Rest your head on your right arm. You may be more comfortable if you put a small pillow or towel under your bent leg.

2 Place the palm of your left hand on your sacrum – the lowest part of your back where the spine connects with the buttocks. On the out-breath, gently press your palm into the sacrum. Release the pressure on the in-breath, then press in again with the next out-breath. Repeat the sequence until the whole area is nicely warmed up.

3 Start to massage your sacrum using the pads of your fingers. Work slowly and precisely, trying to release tension from every spot. Continue for several minutes. If anywhere is sore, roll your knuckles all over the affected area.

4 Roll your knuckles over the left buttock, and down along the left thigh, for three minutes, coming back up to the lower back. Finish by placing the palm of your left hand on the sacrum again, and hold it there for three breaths, imagining that you are breathing toward your sacrum. Turn on your left side and repeat the steps using your right hand.

41

in your
bathroom
soothing

find inner calm by combining
massage with warm water

1 Lie in the bath, and place the index, middle and ring fingers of both hands on your temples. If it is more comfortable, support your head on a pillow. Keep your fingers together, creating a flat surface. Close your eyes and breathe deeply and slowly three times, feeling the connection between your fingers and your temples.

2 (*opposite*) On the out-breath, press the pads of your fingers gradually into your temples, keeping your fingers together and flat. Hold, counting to three. On the in-breath, release the pressure, then start to press into your temples again with your next out-breath, and hold. Repeat three times.

3 Start making another "press-in" sequence, but this time don't release the pressure; instead make five slow, small, precise circles. To avoid stretching your skin, concentrate on moving the tissue underneath, rather than the skin itself.

4 Return to step 2, and make three "press-ins" each time, then three when you hold and make circles. Finish by placing both hands over your face, and breathing deeply.

43

1 (*right*) As you don't need to apply oil or cream for this invigorating massage, you can keep your socks on. Place your left foot on your right knee. Rub the foot between your palms, with your hands moving forward and backward in opposite directions, until your foot is warm.

2 Grasp the toes with your right hand, flexing and extending them rhythmically. Then work on each toe, starting from the big one and squeezing them several times between your thumb and index finger. Apply firm pressure, and make sure that you support the left foot with your left hand all the time you are working on the toes.

3 Work between the tendons on the top of the foot. Using the thumb of your right hand, press between each two toes, then run your finger from their base toward the ankle. Support your foot by holding the ankle with your left hand.

4 Come back to the sole of the left foot. With your fingers supporting your foot from the top, start walking the thumbs of both hands vigorously along the sole. Begin at the top of the sole and walk all the way down, toward the heel. Walk up and down for three minutes. Make sure that you keep the same rhythm all the time. Change over to the other foot, and then repeat all four steps again.

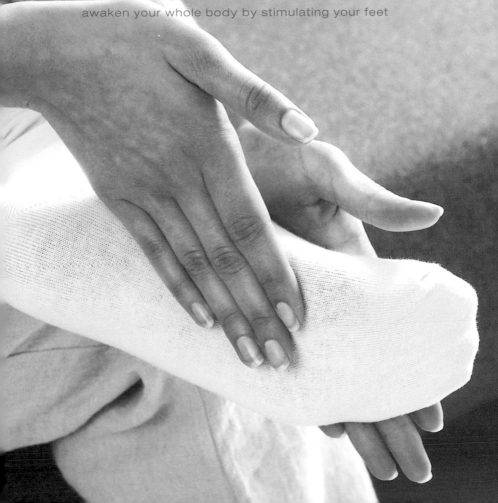

on your sofa
invigorating
awaken your whole body by stimulating your feet

at the park
refreshing

take time out in the open air to refresh your body

1 Sit on a bench or the grass, back supported, legs uncrossed, and hands resting on your lap. Hold your right wrist in your left hand. Rotate your right hand slowly from the wrist, keeping your arm still, five times in one direction and five in another. Drop your hand down and shake it vigorously several times. Repeat with your left hand.

2 Hold your right wrist in your left hand, and, while supporting it with your fingers, lightly press your thumb on the inner, soft part of the wrist, working from the edge of the palm toward the forearm. Hold each pressure for a count of two. Be careful to apply only gentle pressure, as there are lots of blood vessels in this area.

46

3 Squeeze your wrist in your left hand and hold, then move up your arm, squeeze and hold. Work along the forearm until you reach the elbow. Every time you squeeze another part of the forearm, breathe out.

4 Place your right arm along your right thigh, palm facing down. On your out-breath, press the fingers of your left hand into the top of your right wrist. Hold. On the in-breath, move your fingers up along the forearm slightly, press in, and hold while you breathe out. Work all along the forearm. Change arms and repeat steps 1–4.

47

1 Lie down on your back, in a comfortable position, with your arms at your sides and legs slightly apart. If you have a sore lower back, you can place a small pillow or rolled-up towel under your knees to decrease the pressure on the lower part of your spine.

2 (*right*) Place the ball under your neck. Make sure that you don't hold your neck up, but instead let it rest completely on the ball. Breathe deeply, allowing the ball to hold your neck. Try to increase the sensation of sinking your neck into the ball more deeply with each breath.

3 On the out-breath, start to roll your head over the ball, working from the middle to the right and back to the middle. Take in a breath, and when you start to breathe out, roll your head to the left side and back to the middle. Repeat several times, making each movement slow.

4 Change the rhythm, rolling all the way over from left to right on the out-breath, and from right to the left on the in-breath. Work three times in each direction. Don't increase the speed, as you need to be aware of every movement in your neck: it should feel like the space between each vertebra is loosening up. Come back to the neutral position, and breathe deeply, letting your neck rest on the ball.

at the beach
balancing
ease your neck with a massage that
uses a soft, air-filled ball

1 Before you start this massage, try to switch off your mind by closing your eyes and breathing deeply several times. Make sure that your shoulders stay relaxed. Slowly open your eyes and, on your out-breath, press your right thumb firmly but gradually into your left palm. Use the other fingers of your right hand to support the left hand.

2 (*right*) Make three firm, slow circles with your thumb, in both directions, pressing deeply into your palm. Move to any other point, and make another three circles. Make sure that the other fingers of your right hand support the left hand, and that you breathe regularly. Work over the whole palm, then change hands and repeat.

3 Squeeze the index finger of your left hand from its base, between the knuckles of the index and middle finger of your right hand. Pull and twist, right up to your fingertips. Work in the same way on each finger, and then change hands.

4 Lift both your shoulders as close to your ears as possible, and then drop them down. Repeat this movement three times. Return to a neutral position, shoulders relaxed and hands by your sides. Finish by shaking your hands vigorously five times.

at your desk
soothing

release tension from your hands,
and relax your mind

in a hotel room
invigorating
restore your energy between flights and meetings

1 (*left*) Sit straight, your feet flat on the floor. Place a hand either side of your head, fingers spread, little fingers on the hairline at the centre of your forehead. Close your eyes, breathe deeply. On an out-breath, press your palms into your scalp, and slowly lift. Hold for three seconds, then release. Repeat three times.

2 Supporting the left side of your head with your left hand, press your right palm into the right side of your scalp. Moving all over the right side, make circles with your palm. Breathe slowly and regularly, and imagine tension slowly melting away.

3 Change hands, supporting your scalp with your right hand. Press your left palm into the scalp, making circles, as in step 2, over the left side of your scalp.

4 Use the palms of both hands to make circles, lifting and rotating the whole scalp for 30 seconds. Start very slowly, then gradually increase the speed of your circles. Open your eyes. Finish by breathing deeply three times.

53

1 (*right*) While sitting comfortably in your seat, head and shoulders relaxed, place both hands on the tops of your knees, as if you are embracing the knee with your hand. You should feel your kneecap in your palm. Close your eyes and breathe deeply three times.

2 On the next out-breath, make five firm, short circles in an anti-clockwise direction over your knees, using your palms. Stop. Breathe in, and on the next out-breath make another five circles, this time in a clockwise direction. The more vigorously and rhythmically you carry out these movements, the more you will boost your circulation.

3 Try to keep your legs still, but relaxed. Next, tap along the tops of your thighs with the edges of your palms, in an alternating rhythm, working from the knees toward the pelvis, and back to the knees again. Repeat three times.

4 Place both your hands on the tops of your knees again, and then repeat the massage sequences given in steps 1 and 2. Finish with several deep breaths, then hold your hands on your knees for 60 seconds. Open your eyes and slowly release your hands.

on a plane
boosting

help prevent blood-flow stagnating,
especially in your legs and feet

stress
busters

Massage away your stress! You can use massage to help you cope more

easily with physical and emotional problems, and speed up recovery.

A regular, short massage will help you to relax within a couple of

minutes, restoring the whole system.

1   (*right*) Sit in a comfortable postion and place the fingers of both hands along your hairline. Make sure that the little fingers touch each other. With an out-breath, press gently into the hairline and, maintaining pressure, make three circles outward in opposite directions.

2   Place the fingers of each hand along the middle line of your scalp. Make sure that the little fingers are touching the hairline. Breathing out, press gently into the scalp and, as you did on the hairline, make two circles outward in opposite directions with every out-breath.

3   Lift your fingers, and place them further along the middle line. Your little fingers should now be where the index fingers were in step 2. Breathing in, press gently into the scalp and, with an out-breath, make two circles as you did before, taking care to maintain pressure.

4   Move your fingers to the base of your scalp. After the bump at the base, you will feel a little groove. Using your index and middle fingers, press into this area on the out-breath and hold, counting to five. Release, and repeat again. Finish by resting your hands on top of your head, without applying any pressure, and breathing deeply twice.

scalp lifter
relaxing

a scalp massage will release tension
from your face and neck

lower back reliever
soothing

free up lower back muscles and joints, where stress shows first

1 Sit comfortably, legs slightly open. Place your palms each side of the sacrum (lowest part of the back), making sure that you don't press directly on the spine. Rub your palms up and down the sacrum vigorously for 30 seconds, to warm up the muscles. Stop, holding your palms on the sacrum, and breathe in and out three times. Repeat twice.

2 Place the fingers of both hands along both sides of the spine, without pressing directly on the spine. Breathe in, pressing gently into the muscles, and make circles on your out-breath, concentrating on each sore spot. Continue pressing and circling for one minute, breathing regularly.

3 To increase pressure, form a fist and roll your knuckles along your lower back, starting from the sacrum and working up along the spine as high as is comfortable for you.

4 Roll your knuckles down toward your sacrum again, and make slow, firm circles over each buttock. Using the same movement, move to your hip muscles and make five circles with your knuckles. Finish by placing both your palms on the sacrum, and breathing regularly three times.

61

body relaxer
releasing

use deep breathing to release
physical and emotional tension

1 Make sure that your clothing is loose, with no tightness at the waist. Stand or lie down, with both arms relaxed at your sides. Close your eyes and take a deep breath in through your nose, directing it toward your belly. Allow your abdominal muscles to relax. Feel the breath sinking into your body. Exhale through your mouth.

2 (*opposite*) Place whichever hand is most comfortable for you palm down, on your abdomen, with the other hand resting above it. This will help you to direct the breath right there. Continue breathing with closed eyes, and feel your abdomen rise rhythmically with your in-breath, then sink down with the out-breath.

3 Drop your arms back down to your sides and then take another in-breath through your nose. Breathe out naturally, pausing at the end of the out-breath for a second or two before taking another in-breath.

4 Pause for as long as is comfortable and safe for you, and repeat. In the beginning, the pause will probably be very short as you might worry that your body is not filling up with breath. Accept this feeling and allow yourself to explore the pause, relaxing more every time.

eye calmer
refreshing

restore your eyes fast, giving a sense of harmony and peace

1 Sit in a comfortable position, eyes closed, neck and shoulders relaxed. Alternatively, lie with a pillow under your head and another under your knees to improve blood-flow in your legs. Place the fingers of your hands over your eyes. Breathe deeply, and imagine that you are directing every out-breath to your arms, hands and eyes.

2 Remove your hands, and place each middle finger in each inner corner of your eyes. With an out-breath, press gently into each corner with the finger pads, and hold, counting to five. Release, and repeat. Press all over underneath the eyes, holding and counting to five, until you reach the outer corners of your eyes.

64

3 Using your index fingers and thumbs, squeeze the eyebrows above the inner corner of your eyes and hold for five, then release. Work along your eyebrows from the bridge of your nose until you reach your temples, squeezing the eyebrows, then holding, counting to five, and releasing. Repeat.

4 Tap gently under your eyes and over your eyelids, using the finger pads of both hands. This movement should be light and rhythmical. Continue for 30 seconds, then cup both palms over your eyes, breathing deeply three times. Slowly open your eyes.

1 (*right*) Place the index, middle and ring fingers of each hand on each side of your jaw. To be sure that you cover the muscle fully, clench your teeth. You should feel the muscle move under your fingers, which will indicate that you have found the correct position. Close your eyes.

2 Breathe in, and with your out-breath press into the muscle on its highest point, just under the cheek arch, close to the ear lobe. Make five slow circles, pressing with your middle and ring fingers. Breathing regularly, work down along the muscle until you reach the corner of the jaw. Continue making circles as you come back up to the cheek arch. Repeat the sequence three times, keeping your breathing regular.

3 Place your thumbs on the corners of your jaw, fingers resting on your head. Taking a deep breath, open your mouth slightly. As you breathe out, press your thumbs gradually into your jaw, and hold. Slowly release. Repeat three times, feeling the jaw relax more each time.

4 Move to the next point, working with your thumbs from the top of your jaw down to the corners as in step 2, but this time just press and hold for five seconds in each place. Finish by resting your fingers softly along your jaw muscles and breathing deeply three times.

jaw reliever
relaxing

even a short massage
can ease pain and relax your jaw

foot de-stresser releasing

de-stress your body in minutes by stimulating points on your foot

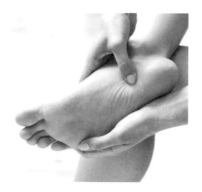 

1 Sit comfortably, and place your right foot on your left knee. Supporting the heel of your foot with your left hand, press into the arch of the foot, using your right thumb. In reflexology, the arch corresponds to the spine, which is the first place to be affected by stress. Make as many small, firm circles as you like all over the arch.

2 Now concentrate on the pad below your big toe, which corresponds to the stomach. Supporting the foot with your left hand, press into the pad with the thumb of your right hand, and make five deep, slow circles.

68

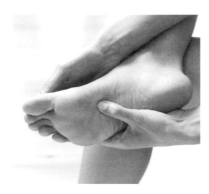

3 Slide your thumb down to the middle of your sole, where a small area corresponds to the kidneys and adrenal glands. Pressing in, make five small, deep circles, still supporting the foot with your left hand.

4 Repeat steps 1–3 in the large area between the middle of your sole and your heel, which relates to the intestines. As a rule, if you find a tender spot it shows that the organ related to that point is under stress. Focus on these areas, breathing deeply, and imagining that you are breathing away tension. Repeat on the other foot.

1 (*right*) Bend your neck forward slightly, and place the middle fingers of both hands in the grooves situated on both sides of your neck vertebrae, at the base of your skull. Don't apply pressure, just breathe deeply and feel the connection between your fingers and your neck.

2 With an out-breath, gradually apply pressure into both grooves (on both sides of your neck vertebrae), using your middle fingers. While pressing, you should bring your neck upright simultaneously, as this will enable you to press into a deeper layer of the muscles.

3 Maintaining pressure, make five circles with your middle fingers, breathing slowly and regularly. Release the pressure gradually, move your fingers slightly apart, and then apply pressure again. Make another five slow, precise circles.

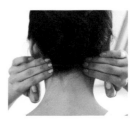

4 Move your fingers sideways along the base of your skull to a new point, with your fingers just underneath the skull bone, and press into the muscles. Make five slow, precise circles, breathing regularly. Gradually release and move your fingers to the next point. Aim to change position five times, until you reach the corner of the bone, just behind your ears. Each time, you should be able to increase the pressure as your neck muscles relax more. Finish by breathing deeply three times.

70

neck **balancer**
unwinding
restore your energy in the middle of the day

mood enhancers

People who feel happy and have a positive approach to life tend to be

healthier than those who are more negative. You will find that simple

self-massage can dramatically lift your mood, slowing down the ageing

process, and bringing joy and vitality into your life.

chest booster uplifting

use this technique to lift your spirits after a disappointment

1 Sit with your neck and shoulders relaxed. Place your right palm on the left side of your chest, close to the shoulder. Make a long, gentle stroke across your chest; sweep off when you reach the right shoulder. Place your left palm on your right chest, and stroke across, sweeping off at the left shoulder. Repeat the whole sequence five times.

2 Place the fingers of both hands along your collarbone. Starting from the middle, make five firm, slow circles. Move to the next point along. Press your fingers in, and make another five circles. Move to another point and continue all along the collarbone until you reach the edge of your shoulder.

3 Make loose fists and rest them gently in the middle of your chest. Press in deeply with both thumbs. Massage between your ribs, using your knuckles to make circles and pressing in with your thumbs all the time. Work all over the chest, breathing regularly.

4 Rest your fists lightly on your chest, but don't press your thumbs in. With an out-breath, tap rhythmically over your chest. Start slowly, gradually increasing speed, while keeping pressure light. Stop to take in breath, and start again with each out-breath. Repeat three times. Finish by placing your hands flat on your chest; breathe deeply twice.

75

foot reviver
boosting

a super-fast mood reviver, as feet connect to all your organs

1 Sit on a chair, with your right foot resting on your left knee. Alternatively, you can sit cross-legged on the floor if that is comfortable for you. If you can't get your foot on top of your left knee, rest it on the floor in front of your knee. Keep your back straight and relaxed.

2 Place the toes of your right foot between both palms, making a sandwich. Rub the toes, moving your palms forward and backward in a fast, rhythmical way. Continue for at least 30 seconds, or until you start to feel a warmth in the upper part of your foot.

3 (*left*) Move to the middle part of the foot. Squeeze the middle of the sole and the top of the foot gently between both palms, and start to rub vigorously. You can vary the speed, increasing and decreasing gradually. Continue for 30 seconds, or until you feel warmth spreading from the foot to the upper leg.

4 Support the ankle of the right foot with your right hand. Place your left palm along the sole of the right foot, and rub along the whole sole vigorously, from the heel up to the toes. Continue for at least 30 seconds. Change over to the other foot and repeat steps 1–4.

77

1 Sit or lie down. Lift your hands to your face, but make sure that you don't lift your shoulders – keep them relaxed all the time. Place the fingers of both hands on your forehead. Press gradually into the tissue, and make as many circles as you need to cover your forehead. It is important that you don't slide over the skin, stretching it unnecessarily, but rather move the tissue, which lies underneath.

2 (*right*) Continue making circles for 30 seconds, then move to the cheeks. Press your fingers against the cheekbones and make circles without stretching the skin. Continue for 30 seconds, then move to the jaw, pressing into the jawbone, before you start to make five circles.

3 Place both palms over your face, and, keeping them loose, make light, upward strokes, starting from the jaw line and sweeping off on the forehead. You can create an uplifting sensation very quickly if you keep to light, rhythmical strokes.

4 Using the pads of the fingers of both hands, tap all over your face gently, starting on the forehead, then working lightly around your eyes, and slightly more firmly on the cheeks and jaw. Start slowly, increasing the speed gradually. The movement should be like light rain drops.

face lifter
restoring

release tension from your
face to restore your spirits

abdominal soother
balancing

massage your abdomen to leave you calmer and more tranquil

1 For maximum relaxation, carry out this massage unclothed, using some massage oil. Lie down and place your hands on your abdomen, palms down. Breathe deeply. Feel your abdomen rising and sinking with your in- and out-breath. Try to be aware of your the effects on your mood – you should feel calmer and more relaxed.

2 Stroke your abdomen with one hand after another, working in a clockwise direction and maintaining the constant flow of the movement as you gently lift and replace the hands.

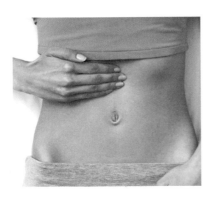

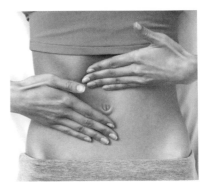

3 Use the fingers of your right hand to make small circles all around your abdomen, following its outline in a clockwise direction. These circles should connect with your breathing. If you want to, place one hand on the top of the other and increase the pressure to reach a deeper layer of muscle.

4 Press both palms flat across the lowest part of your abdomen, and stroke alternately upward, along your middle. While one hand is sweeping off below your chest, the other hand starts stroking upward from below your navel, maintaining a rhythmic, flowing movement. Finish by repeating step 1.

81

head **booster**
invigorating

whisk away your low mood with a stimulating massage

1 Sit, feet connected with the floor. Breathe deeply, feeling energy coming from your feet and travelling toward your hands. Place your hands on each side of your head, fingers pointing upward. On an out-breath press your hands slowly toward each other. Hold, count to three, and slowly release. Repeat three times.

2 Using relaxed, curled fingers, make circles all over your scalp. Keep your fingers firmly in place so that you move the skin against the bone. You shouldn't be able to hear any sound of the hair rubbing against the scalp. Make every circular movement dynamic and invigorating.

3 Support your head with your left hand and, using the flat fingers of your right hand, rub lightly and vigorously all over the surface of your scalp. Rub backward and forward, up and across, making sure that you cover the whole of your head.

4 (opposite) Continue rubbing backward and forward, but this time use the palms of both hands at the same time, and rub all over the scalp, starting from the hairline and finishing on the base of the scalp. Maintain the speed and dynamism of the movement throughout.

neck warmer unwinding

free up communication by easing stiffness in your neck

1 Stand or sit, and relax your shoulders. Make alternate strokes down your neck, starting from the back of your head and sweeping off on the back of the shoulders. When one hand reaches the shoulder, the other should start the stroke from the back of the head. Keep the flow going, and you will start to feel the muscles warming up.

2 Place your left hand over the left side of the neck for support, and bend the head slightly. Place the edge of your right palm against the base of your skull, and rub lightly but vigorously up and down, all over the base of the scalp, starting from the middle and going out toward the ear, and maintaining a constant rhythm throughout.

3 Supporting the head with the left hand, spread the thumb and fingers of the right hand around the neck. Squeeze the neck between your thumb and fingers, starting from the base of the scalp and going down to the base of the neck. Repeat three times.

4 When you reach the base of the neck, grasp the flesh there between thumb and fingers and pull it back. Slide to the middle of the neck, grasp flesh again and pull it back. Then slide to the base of the skull, grasp and pull flesh again. Repeat steps 3 and 4, changing hands and using the right hand to support and the left one to massage.

85

1 (*right*) Sit comfortably, with your neck relaxed and your head slightly bent. Place the middle fingers of both hands under your cheekbones on each side of the nose. There are shiatsu points located here, one on either side of the nose, which relate to the sinuses.

2 On the out-breath, gradually start to apply pressure. You can press quite strongly as long as you find it comfortable. Hold, counting to five, while you breathe in. On an out-breath, slowly release the pressure. Repeat the whole sequence three times. Move your fingers to another spot along the cheekbone, toward the ear, and apply pressure again. Repeat the sequence in the next spot along, until you reach your ear.

3 Next, unless you're pregnant, find the shiatsu headache spot, between your thumb and index finger. Locate the point by pressing around until you get a distinctive feeling. Press your right-hand thumb into your left palm several times, holding, and counting to five.

4 Change hands, and repeat step 3, pressing the left-hand thumb into the right palm. Then repeat the nasal and the hand acupressure sequences (steps 1–2 and step 3) one more time. Finish by cupping the palms of both hands over your face and breathing deeply three times.

sinus
clearer
restoring

open up your sinuses,
reducing headaches

energy
boosters

Massage is the best stimulant ever! When you feel that your energy

levels are dropping, instead of reaching for the coffee or the sugary

snacks, just spend five minutes on one of these techniques. You will

speed up your circulation, tone your muscles, and revitalize your

energy immediately, so you can face the world again.

1 Sit up straight and embrace yourself by placing your palms, with your fingers widely spread, as high up as possible on both outsides of your arms. Press your palms and fingers firmly into the upper arm muscles. Breathe out, squeezing and slowly massaging the muscles using your fingers and the middle edges of your palms.

2 Slide your hands down your arms, and embrace yourself just above the elbows. On the out-breath, squeeze the muscles and slowly massage them. Use your fingers for massaging the outer part of the muscles, and your thumbs for massaging the inner part. Repeat steps 1 and 2 three times, massaging your arms in both positions each time.

3 Embrace yourself, reaching as far as you can. On the out-breath, slowly stretch out your shoulderblades without lifting them. At the same time, bend your head slowly, creating stretch along the spine and between the shoulderblades. Hold for a count of five, and slowly release.

4 (*right*) Place your arms behind your back, holding the right wrist with the left hand. Breathing out, slowly stretch your shoulders as far back as is comfortable, opening the chest and collarbones. Try to feel the shoulderblades touching each other. Hold for a count of five; release.

shoulder stretcher
reinvigorating
massage and stretches release tension from your upper back

face booster uplifting

acupressure restores energy flow all over your body

1 Lie down, with one small pillow under your knees and a second under your neck. Rest for a while, eyes closed, and arms by your sides. Breathe deeply. With every breath try to relax your body and mind more deeply.

2 Place your right-hand middle finger just below your hairline, in the middle of your forehead. With an out-breath, press in, using the pad of your finger. On the next out-breath make five slow, small circles in one direction. Stop, take a breath, and as you breathe out make five circles in the opposite direction. Move down and repeat.

3 The next point is slightly below the middle of your forehead. Press in while you take a breath and, on the out-breath, make five circles in one direction. Breathe in and press, then on the out-breath make five circles in the other direction. Slide down to the next point, between the eyebrows, press in gradually and repeat the sequence.

4 You will find the last two points on the nose. Starting in the middle, where there is a little groove, repeat the slow breathing, pressing and circling sequence. Then apply the sequence to the final point, on the tip of your nose. Don't worry if you can't find the point at first. With practice, your fingers will locate its energy-flow easily.

93

1

Sit straight, or stand. Place both hands on either side of the neck, where it connects to the shoulders. Don't apply any pressure yet. Just hold your hands, close your eyes, and breathe deeply three times, feeling the connection between your hands and the base of your neck.

2

(*right*) Bend your head back, and squeeze the muscles on each side of the base of the neck with your fingers and thumbs. The amount of muscle you are able to grasp will depend on how tense your neck and shoulders are. If you can't squeeze any portion of the muscles, just press your palms against the muscles as firmly as you can.

3

Slowly roll your head forward on an out-breath, squeezing the muscles all the time. You'll feel a nice stretch between the shoulder tops and the base of your neck. Bend your head forward as far as you can, squeezing the muscles. Hold, counting to ten and breathing deeply.

4

Slowly, return your head to the upright position. Next, repeat steps 2 and 3 twice, returning your head to the upright position between each sequence. Finally, finish the massage by placing both your palms flat, on either side of your neck, and breathing deeply.

94

neck reviver
restoring

a great break when you feel that
your energy level is dropping

thigh booster
reviving

improve your blood and energy flow after sitting for a long time

1 Sit straight, with your legs slightly open. Place the palms of both hands on the top of your right thigh and warm up the muscles by making long, vigorous strokes along the thigh, up and down. Keep the strokes rhythmical.

2 Form fists with both hands and place them on top of the right thigh. Press thumbs into the top of the thigh for better support, and make circles using your knuckles. Work all over the top of the thigh, then on the inner and outer part as well. Keep the movement dynamic, and breathe deeply.

3 Place your flat palms on the top of the thigh and lift your fingertips so only the middle of the edges of the palms are touching your leg. Tap all over the thigh, using the edges of both palms, and working up and down, covering the top, inner and outer parts of the thigh. Try altering the speed and pressure.

4 Place the middle edge of your right palm just above your right knee and massage firmly, using circular pressure. Place your left hand on the inner part of the right knee for support. Carry this out this much more slowly than previous steps, making sure that your breathing is regular and deep. Repeat on your left thigh.

97

ear reviver
stimulating

working on reflex points in your
ears energizes your whole body

1 This is one of the easiest massages; you can practise it while you are sitting, standing, or lying down. If you are wearing earrings, remove them before you start. Close your eyes. Make sure that you breathe regularly during the massage.

2 Squeeze your ears between your thumbs and first two fingers. Starting at the lobe base, press, squeeze and knead until your scalp feels warm. Walk your fingers up around the outside to the top of your ear, massaging firmly as you go. Return to the lobe, squeezing between thumb and two fingers for a count of five.

3 (*left*) Twiddle your ears, using your thumbs and index fingers, and in the same direction and over the same area as in step 2. Do this three times. Your ears should feel hot now, and you might even experience a tingling sensation over your ears and face – a sign of free energy-flow.

4 Squeezing the tops of your ears between your thumbs and index fingers, pull up on your ears gently and rhythmically five times. Finish by squeezing the lobe between your thumbs and index fingers and pulling down gently and rhythmically five times. Open your eyes.

1 Stand with your legs slightly open. Make sure that your knees are not locked, as this would disturb the energy flow. Close your eyes. Place your hands, palms down, on both sides of your lower back. Hold gently, and send the breath toward your back. With every breath, feel the tension releasing slowly. Keep your eyes closed.

2 (*right*) Form tight fists with both hands, and start to tap vigorously, but not very fast, along both sides of your lower back between the vertebrae, using both fists at the same time. Set a consistent rhythm, and make sure that you don't tap over your spine.

3 Continue tapping, and move out from the middle of your lower back toward the hips. Spend extra time on both buttocks, tapping firmly and vigorously. Make sure that the buttock muscles are relaxed and your wrists are loose. Breathe regularly.

4 Return to the middle of the lower back, tapping all the time. Move up toward the shoulders, tapping both sides of the back, either side of the spine, as high as is comfortable for you. Work up and down your back three times, and then repeat the sequence, starting at step 2, twice.

back
releaser
invigorating

unlock the reservoir of energy
locked in your lower back

body energizer
boosting

use one technique to supply your whole body with fresh energy

 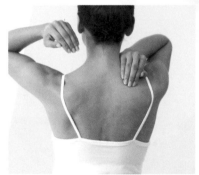

1 Stand with your arms relaxed and eyes closed, and breathe deeply several times. Open your eyes, and, starting from the shoulder and moving down to the hand, cup your left arm rhymically with the palm of your right hand. Move to a steady rhythm, and match your breathing to this. Repeat three times, change arm, and start again.

2 Using your right palm, cup vigorously along your left shoulder as far back as you can reach, for 15 seconds. Do the same on the other shoulder, using your left palm. Make sure that you maintain the rhythm, and that your wrist stays loose. It is important that you use cupping only on the fleshy areas, avoiding bony parts.

3 Move down to either side of your waist, and start cupping, first along your waist, then down along the hips, and up again toward the waist. Make sure that you stay on the sides of your body, avoiding the front, which is the site of all your organs.

4 Using both palms, cupping alternately, work on your legs, one at a time, covering the top, both sides, and the back of the thigh. Work vigorously for at least 15 seconds. Move to the lower leg. Concentrate on the back of the calf as the front is mostly bone. Cup in a steady rhythm for at least 15 seconds. Repeat on the other leg.

practising together

Massage is such a great way to show affection, respect and love. Don't wait for a long holiday to reward each other with healing touch. Practise these techniques as often as possible, bearing in mind that giving a massage can be as beneficial as receiving one.

1 (*right*) Stand in front of each other, knees slightly bent, and arms at your sides. Close your eyes and breathe deeply. Be aware of your partner's presence. Slowly reach for their hands without opening your eyes. Hold them for a moment, then while your partner keeps their hands still, start to explore the hands' shape and texture, using your fingers and thumbs. Imagine you have never touched them before.

2 Move very slowly and carefully, as if you are touching a precious, fragile object. Take as much time as you need. This will help you to maintain a light touch, which will give much more sensation than firm pressure. Now it is your partner's turn to try steps 1 and 2 on you.

3 It is your turn. Place both palms gently over your partner's face, without opening your eyes. Starting from the forehead, explore their face with your fingers. Look for signs of tension. Move over eyes and cheeks, then down to jaw and ears. Try to guess what this face wants "to tell you".

4 Allow your partner to discover your face while you are just present, open to receiving their touch. Be aware of sensations in your body. What kind of feelings surface? Finish by looking into each other's eyes, holding hands, and breathing together three times.

getting
connected
exploring

re-discover each other simply through touch

letting go
reviving

give your partner a shoulder massage when they arrive home

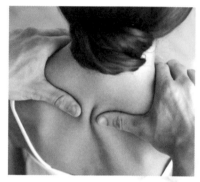

1 Ask your partner to sit in a chair, feet flat on floor, hands in their lap. Stand behind them, and place your left palm on their left shoulder and your right one on their right shoulder. Tell your partner to close their eyes and breathe deeply three times. Breathe deeply too, feeling the connection between your hands and their shoulders.

2 Squeeze the shoulder muscles between your fingers and thumbs, using as much of your hands as possible in order to avoid pinching your partner's skin. Lift and roll the muscles alternately, one side at a time, between your fingers and thumb.

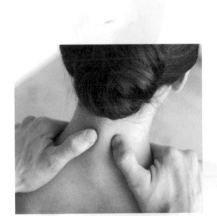

3 Place your thumbs either side of your partner's spine at the base of the neck, in the grooves between the vertebrae. Slowly press into these points simultaneously, and release. Move your thumbs down to the next space. Press again. Release slowly. Move down again, and repeat. Work along the spine, never pressing on it directly.

4 Standing to your partner's right side, reach across their chest to their left shoulder, placing one arm in front and the other behind. Interlock your fingers around their shoulder and squeeze the muscle between your palms. Hold for a count of five; release. Repeat, pressing into the middle of the shoulder. Repeat step 4 on the other shoulder.

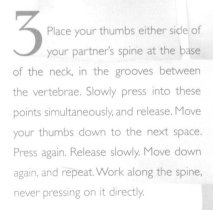

109

1 While your partner is sitting down in a chair or on the floor, stand or kneel directly behind them and place both your hands on their shoulders. Ask them to breathe deeply as this will calm them down and help to release the tension that is stored in their back muscles.

2 Move to your left, and press your right palm edge into the muscles along the right side of your partner's lower back. As you press in, push the muscles away. Work over the lower back without pressing directly on the spine. Change sides, working in the same way on the left side.

3 Stand behind your partner again and, working where the tailbone is situated, using both thumbs, press into the muscles either side of the spine. Press into the muscles on your partner's out-breath, and release the pressure when they

are breathing in. Alternatively you can hold the pressure each time, counting to five, while your partner breathes deeply and regularly.

4 (*right*) With your left hand supporting your partner's back, apply circular pressure with the palm of your right hand on the lower part of the back. Strokes can be firm and vigorous, warming up the muscles and improving the blood circulation. Avoid putting pressure directly on the spine. Finish by placing both hands on your partner's shoulders again.

110

back relaxer
de-stressing

release your partner's tense muscles,
bringing harmony and calm

working together
restoring

at the end of the day, restore the bond between you both

1 (left) Sit on the floor, back to back, spines touching, legs comfortably crossed, and hands palms down on your knees. If you find the floor uncomfortable, you can sit on two small stools. If this is your choice, make sure that you sit with your feet flat on the floor, shoulders relaxed, and hands on your knees. Close your eyes.

2 Adjust your position against your partner's back, sitting straight so that you don't feel that you are leaning into each other too much. Without talking, start to breathe deeply, feeling your partner's presence.

3 Concentrate on your own breathing, directing your breath toward your abdomen. Be aware of all the thoughts passing through your mind and let them go. Observe the movement of the muscles in your back and belly while you are breathing. Stay in close connection with your partner's spine.

4 When you feel connected with your own body rhythm, tune in to your partner's breathing. Try to feel the movement of their back muscles, and follow the rhythm of your partner's breath. Feel their presence through their breath, and the gentle movement of their spine.

113

sleep enhancer
relaxing

wish someone good night with a short face massage

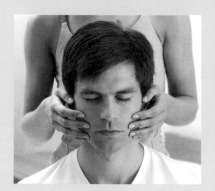 

1 Sit your partner on a chair and stand behind them, placing your hands gently on their head. Make sure that you don't apply any pressure with your hands, just hold. Ask your partner to breathe deeply three times. Now place both hands over their face, and make five gentle, light strokes from the middle of the face to either side.

2 Place the fingers of both hands flat on your partner's temples. Press in, and make five circles upward. It is important that you maintain pressure while you make circles, to avoid stretching the skin. You should make your circles very slow, concentrating on the layer of muscle under the skin.

114

3 Change position, moving your hands to your partner's jaw. Press into the muscles behind their teeth with your flat fingers, and make five small, firm circles. The jaw muscle is one of the body's strongest, so don't be afraid to apply firm pressure.

4 Using the fingers of both hands, stroke one hand after the other up the forehead, into the hairline. Stroke rhythmically, making sure that your hands are relaxed. Repeat five times: the repetitive movement is what makes the stroke so relaxing. Place your hands gently on your partner's head, and breathe together three times.

115

SLEEP ENHANCER

1 (*right*) Sit comfortably, facing each other. Take your partner's right hand and hold it in both your hands, while your partner breathes deeply. Place your hands either side of your partner's right lower arm. Squeeze and release the muscles using your hands alternately, working down to the wrist and then up again toward the elbow. Repeat three times.

2 Hold your partner's right hand between the fingers and thumbs of both your hands, sliding your thumbs over and gradually stretching out the top of their right hand with the edges of your thumbs. Repeat this three times, holding each hand stretch for three seconds.

3 Turn your partner's hand so that the palm is facing up. Place your left little finger between your partner's thumb and index finger, and your right little finger between the little and ring finger of your partner's hand. The rest of your fingers should be underneath your partner's hand.

4 At the same time, press down with your thumbs and up with your fingers, so that the palm stretches out slightly. Repeat three times, trying each time to achieve a deeper stretch in your partner's palm. Then use the thumbs to massage the palm, making five small, firm circles. Repeat steps 1–4 on your partner's left arm and hand.

touching hands
soothing

hands

show love and respect to your
partner with a hand massage

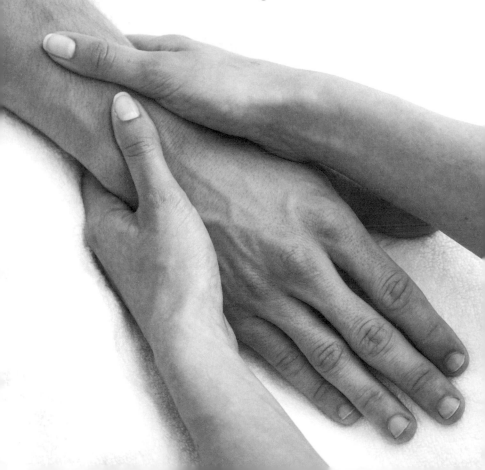

caring for feet
pampering

friends will be grateful for a relaxing, soothing foot massage

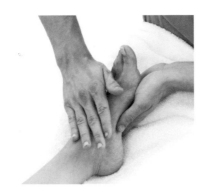

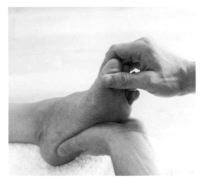

1 Hold your partner's left foot on your lap while you both sit comfortably, facing each other. Support the sole of your partner's foot with your left hand, and make long, rhythmical strokes over the top of their foot with the palm of your right hand. Stroke your hand rhythmically from their toes toward their ankle, warming up the foot.

2 Still supporting the foot with your left hand, squeeze your partner's big toe between the fingers and thumb of your right hand, and make five firm circles. Move to the second toe and repeat the sequence. Work on the other three toes one by one.

118

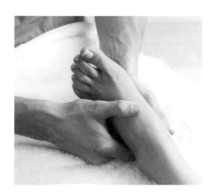 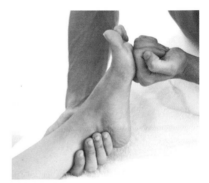

3 Slide the thumb of your right hand along the tendons, from the knuckle of the big toe toward the ankle, while your left hand supports the sole of your partner's left foot. Repeat, working from every toe along the tendon.

4 Form a fist with your left hand and slide it very slowly along the sole of your partner's foot, from the base of their toes to the heel. Hold the top of your partner's foot with your right hand, so that you can press against the top of their foot while you slide over the sole with your left fist. Change foot, and then repeat steps 1–4.

119

balancing
touch
caring

head massage is especially beneficial,
so offer a caring touch

1 (*left*) Ask your partner to lie down, head on the bed's edge. Sit on a chair, behind their head. Place both palms under their head, so they feel supported. Ask them to breathe deeply, and on an out-breath press your fingers under their scalp bone, where the neck connects. Hold, and slowly release. Repeat three times.

2 With your partner's head resting in your hands, lift it slightly, and drop it into your hands without any resistance. You should be able to feel its heaviness. Hold, counting to five. Lift a little more, then hold, counting to five, and lift even more, holding and counting to five. Slowly, gradually, lower the head back.

3 Slide your palms gently out from underneath your partner's head, place them on either side of their head and apply very light pressure. This can be very relaxing if you do it for at least 30 seconds.

4 Spread your fingers, and massage your partner's scalp with your finger pads. Press into the tissue first, then make at least ten slow, small circles. Ensure that you are moving the tissue underneath, rather than just rubbing the skin. Finish by holding your palms on either side of your partner's head for ten seconds.

121

tension reliever releasing

offer to release tension in your partner's neck and shoulders

1 Ask your partner to sit comfortably, with their feet flat on the floor. Standing on their left, place your left hand on their forehead and stroke their neck with your right palm. Using long movements, start from the base of the neck and work down toward their shoulders. Your partner should feel a warmth over the neck area.

2 Supporting your partner's head with your left hand, hold their neck between your right-hand thumb and fingers. Make five circles with your thumb and fingers, moving from the base of the neck to the base of the scalp, back down and up again. Maintain a rhythm and keep the movement slow and gentle, as the neck can be sensitive.

122

3 When you reach the base of the scalp, continue making small circles with your thumb and the rest of your fingers on either side of your partner's head. Work out along the base of the scalp toward the ears in slow motion, until you reach the corner of the scalp bone, behind the ears.

4 When you reach the corner of the bone, come back to the middle point and start again, working in circles toward the ears. Repeat three times. Finish by covering the whole area of your partner's neck with the palm of your right hand. Hold for 30 seconds.

123

everyday sequences

If you are looking for a massage sequence when you have a little more time, use these menus to select the best one for you — soothing or invigorating, relaxing or energizing. You can try these massages in any suitable location.

half-hour unwinder	half-hour calmer	half-hour uplifter
32 take a moment	64 eye calmer	102 body energizer
66 jaw reliever	30 lazy weekend	74 chest booster
70 neck balancer	28 evening de-stress	36 at a conference
62 body relaxer	42 in your bathroom	82 head booster
60 lower back reliever	40 in your bedroom	44 on a sofa

one hour de-stress

62 body relaxer
64 eye calmer
78 face lifter
58 scalp lifter
66 jaw reliever
84 neck warmer
50 at your desk
68 foot de-stresser
40 in your bedroom

one hour reviver

102 body energizer
22 morning wake-up
100 back releaser
96 thigh booster
26 lunchtine lift
52 in a hotel room
92 face booster
86 sinus clearer
54 before a meeting
46 at a park
76 neck reviver

one hour energy booster

102 body energizer
92 face booster
52 in a hotel room
98 ear reviver
94 neck reviver
26 lunchtime energizer
90 shoulder stretcher
100 back releaser
96 thigh booster
44 on a sofa
46 at the park

index

abdominal soother 80–1

baby massage 8
back
  lower back massage 40–1
  lower back reliever 60–1,
    124
  relaxer 110–11
  releaser 100–1, 125
balancing massage
  abdominal soother 80–1
  at the beach 48–9
  before a meeting 34–5, 125
balancing touch 120–1
bathroom, in your 42–3, 124
beach, at the 48–9
bedroom, in your 40–1, 124,
  125
body energizer 102–3, 124,
  125
body relaxer 62–3, 124, 125
boosting massage
  body energizer 102–3, 124,
    125
  foot reviver 76–7
  on a plane 54–5

breathing 15, 16, 19
  body relaxer 62–3, 124,
    125

calming massage, half-hour
  calmer 124
caring for feet 118–19
caring massage, balancing
  touch 120–1
chest booster 74–5, 124
conference, at a 36–7, 124
connecting massage, shower
  time 24–5
contra-indications for massage
  13–14
couples 10

desk, at your 50–1, 125
de-stressing massage
  back relaxer 110–11
  in your bedroom 40–1, 124,
    125
  one hour de-stress 125

"each other" massage
  techniques 10–11

ear reviver 98–9, 125
energizing massage, lunchtime
  lift 26–7, 125
energy boosters 88–103
  back releaser 100–1, 125
  body energizer 102–3, 124,
    125
  ear reviver 98–9, 125
  face booster 92–3, 125
  neck reviver 94–5, 125
  shoulder stretcher 90–1, 125
  thigh booster 96–7, 125
evening de-stress 28–9, 124
exploring massage, getting
  connected 106–7
eye calmer 64–5, 124, 125

face massage
  face booster 92–3, 125
  face lifter 78–9, 125
  in your bathroom 42–3, 124
  sleep enhancer 114–15
focusing massage, take a
  moment 32–3, 124
foot massage
  caring for feet 118–19

evening de-stress 28–9, 124
foot de-stresser 68–9, 125
on your sofa 44–5, 124, 125
foot reviver 76–7

getting connected 106–7

half-hour sequences 124
hand massage
at the park 46–7, 125
at your desk 50–1, 125
lazy weekend 30–1, 124
touching hands 116–17
head massage
balancing touch 120–1
head booster 82–3, 124
scalp lifter 58–9, 125
healing and massage 6–8
hotel room, in a 54–5, 125

invigorating massage
back releaser 100–1, 125
head booster 82–3, 124
in a hotel room 54–5, 125
morning wake up 22–3, 125
on your sofa 44–5, 124, 125

jaw reliever 66–7, 124, 125

lazy weekend 30–1, 124
leg massage, on a plane 54–5
letting go 108–9
lower back reliever 60–1, 124
lunchtime lift 26–7, 125

meeting, before a 34–5, 125
mood enhancers 72–87
abdominal soother 80–1
chest booster 74–5, 124
face lifter 67–9, 125
foot reviver 76–7
head booster 82–3, 124
neck warmer 84–5, 125
sinus clearer 86–7, 125
morning wake-up 22–3, 125

neck massage
at the beach 48–9
neck balancer 70–1, 124
neck reviver 94–5, 125
neck warmer 84–5, 125
tension reliever 122–3

one hour sequences 125

pain 16
pampering massage
caring for feet 118–19
lazy weekend 30–1, 124
park, at the 46–7, 125
plane, on a 54–5
pregnancy 13

refreshing massage
at a conference 36–7, 124
at the park 46–7, 125
eye calmer 64–5, 124, 125
reinvigorating massage,
shoulder stretcher 90–1, 125
relaxing massage
jaw reliever 66–7, 124, 125
scalp lifter 58–9, 125
sleep enhancer 114–15
releasing massage
body relaxer 62–3, 124, 125
foot de-stresser 68–9, 125
tension reliever 122–3
restoring massage
face lifter 78–9, 125

neck reviver 94–5, 125
sinus clearer 86–7, 125
working together 112–13
reviving massage
  letting go 108–9
  thigh booster 96–7, 125
rhythm 16–19

scalp lifter 58–9, 125
senior massage 8–10
shoulder massage 36–7
  giving to a partner 108–9
  tension reliever 122–3
shoulder stretcher 90–1, 125
shower time 24–5
silence 15–16
sinus clearer 86–7, 125
sleep enhancer 114–15

sleep patterns, evening
  de-stress 28–9, 124
sofa, on your 44–5, 124, 125
soothing massage
  at your desk 50–1, 125
  evening de-stress 28–9, 124
  lower back reliever 60–1,
    124
  in your bathroom 42–3, 124
speed of massage 16–19
stimulating massage, ear reviver
  98–9, 125
stress busters 56–71
  body relaxer 62–3, 124, 125
  eye calmer 64–5, 124, 125
  foot de-stresser 68–9, 125
  jaw reliever 66–7, 124, 125
  lower back reliever 60–1

neck balancer 70–1, 124
scalp lifter 58–9, 125

take a moment 32–3, 124
teenagers 10
tension reliever 122–3
thigh booster 96–7, 125
touching hands 116–17

unwinding massage
  half-hour unwinder 124
  neck warmer 84–5, 125
uplifting massage
  chest booster 74–5, 124
  face booster 92–3, 125
  half-hour uplifter 124

working together 112–13

acknowledgments

author's acknowledgments

I would like to thank Duncan Baird for giving me such a fantastic opportunity to share my thoughts and experience on touch with others, Grace Cheetham for inspiration, enthusiasm and real support, Judith More for guiding me through the complexity of the English language and for such wonderful editing, Manisha Patel for making the book look so beautiful, and my son Igor and my husband Jean-Marc for their love and for believing in me.

publisher's acknowledgments

Duncan Baird Publishers would like to thank models Sarina Carruthers and Adam Mommsen, hair and make-up artist Tinks Reding, and photographer's assistant Adam Giles.